# Animals in the Wild

# Tiger

## by Mary Hoffman

## Windward/Belitha Press

This little cub is as pretty and as playful
as a tabby kitten. But one day it will be
a powerful killer. It will be the biggest of
the big cats and the most feared. It will be

a tiger! Look at its enormous teeth and its
fierce snarl. But even at its most frightening,
the tiger is still one of the most beautiful
wild animals. It is one of the strongest too.

But like all cats, tigers are born small, blind
and helpless. They rely on their mother for food
and protection. Two or more cubs are born
in a litter. The white spots behind their ears

may help their mother to see them in the grass.
By the third week, the cubs can see clearly.
When they are six weeks old they are ready
to go with their mother when she makes a kill.

While they live with their mother, she must
teach the cubs to kill animals for their food.
Their father doesn't help to bring them up.
The mother tiger won't have any more cubs
until these are able to hunt for themselves.

Growing tigers are hungry creatures. First
their mother kills animals for them to eat.
Then they practise hunting animals such as
small wild pigs. When they are grown up,
tigers catch about thirty big animals a year.

Cubs stay with their mother almost two years.
After that they live and hunt on their own.
When a tiger cub is ready to leave the litter, it
must find its own territory. It needs a big
space to live in – about thirty square miles.

Not all tigers live in the jungle. They don't
mind frost and can walk easily through the snow
on their big paws. Tigers probably came first
from the cold North and some still live in snowy
places, like Siberia and the Himalayas.

All tigers have striped coats and bars on their
faces but not all are the same colour.
This rare white tiger is found in India. Its
silvery fur is striped with black. Siberian
tigers have long, pale fur with brown stripes.

When we think of tigers, it is usually the Bengal ones with their bright orange coats and black stripes. Unlike lions, tigers don't have manes, but the old males have long cheek fur. And look at those magnificent whiskers!

If you live in a forest and the light flickers
through the trees, it is very useful to have
a striped coat. A tiger can be almost invisible;
its stripes give it perfect camouflage.

Stripes also make good camouflage when the tiger wants a rest in the long grass. If it starts stalking, it will be very hard to see. It spends most of the day resting and hunts at night.

The tiger can run very fast. But some of the
animals it likes to eat can run even faster.
So it has to creep up on them slowly and then
put on a final burst of speed before it springs.

This one is catching a bird – not much of a meal for a hungry tiger. Although tigers mainly eat deer and wild pigs, they will hunt anything. But tigers usually attack people only if they are frightened.

One of the few wild animals the tiger has to fear is the crocodile. When a tiger goes down to drink in a river, a crocodile may pull it into the water and hold it under until it drowns.

Tigers love the water. They are among the few
cats who really enjoy a swim. In hot places
like India, tigers take to rivers to cool off.
They must have water in their territory.

There are few tigers left now. Too many have been killed for sport. But this man Arjan Singh has made a safe home for tigers in India.

This cub Tara has come to live there. She will get plenty to eat and no-one will shoot or trap her. Tara is luckier than most tigers.

First published 1983 by Windward

An imprint owned by
W. H. Smith & Son Limited
Registered No 237811 England
Trading as WHS Distributors, St. John's House,
East Street, Leicester LE1 6NE

by arrangement with Belitha Press Ltd
40 Belitha Villas, London N1 1PD

Dedicated to Phyllis Hoffman

Scientific Adviser: Dr Gwynne Vevers
Picture Researcher: Stella Martin
Designer: Julian Holland

Acknowledgements are due to Bruce Coleman Ltd
for all photographs in this book with the following
exceptions: Jacana Ltd Cover, pp 4, 11; Eric Hosking p 14;
Natural History Photographic Agency pp 8-9

Printed by W. S. Cowell Ltd
8 Butter Market, Ipswich, Suffolk